This book belongs to

....

It was given to me by

....

On this date

....

ESTHER & ME
Devotions for Girls

Trisha Priebe

BARBOUR **kidz**
A Division of Barbour Publishing

To Avy, Willow, Claire, and Jillian.

Wise women stand with courage
and do what's right no matter the cost.

May you know them, love them, follow them, be them.

© 2023 by Barbour Publishing, Inc.

ISBN 978-1-63609-620-9

All rights reserved. No part of this publication may be reproduced or transmitted for commercial purposes, except for brief quotations in printed reviews, without written permission of the publisher. Reproduced text may not be used on the World Wide Web.

Churches and other noncommercial interests may reproduce portions of this book without the express written permission of Barbour Publishing, provided that the text does not exceed 500 words and that the text is not from material quoted from another publisher. When reproducing text this book, include the following credit line: "From *Esther & Me: Devotions for Girls*, published by Barbour Publishing, Inc. Used by permission."

All scripture quotations are taken from the New Life Version copyright © 1969 and 2003 by Barbour Publishing, Inc., Uhrichsville, Ohio 44683. All rights reserved.

Cover illustrations by Pedro Riquelme

Published by Barbour Publishing, Inc., 1810 Barbour Drive, Uhrichsville, Ohio 44683, www.barbourbooks.com

Our mission is to inspire the world with the life-changing message of the Bible.

Printed in China.
001652 0723 DS

Welcome to
Esther & Me
Devotions for Girls!

In the Bible, whenever God's special people were in trouble, He would often send something miraculous to save them. Sometimes it was armies. At other times it might be frogs or floods.

In this story—one of the most exciting stories in the Old Testament—God doesn't send a miracle. He didn't even send a man. God sent a young woman named Esther.

She was a very pretty girl. And she was just as beautiful on the inside as she was on the outside. Esther risked her own life for the sake of her Jewish people. And she changed history.

Journey with Esther as she grows from an orphan girl to the protector of her people. Keep your eye on the bad guy, Haman. Attend a beauty contest that brings Esther to the king's palace. And search for clues that God is writing the story from beginning to end.

Most important, learn how every detail of Esther's life was arranged by God for "such a time as this." That's true for you too!

ORPHAN GIRL

THE SAD BEGINNING

[Mordecai] had brought up Hadassah, that is Esther, the daughter of his father's brother. For she did not have a father or mother. The young lady was beautiful in body and face.

ESTHER 2:7

Here is the story of Esther—one of the strangest and most exciting adventures in the Old Testament.

Only two books in the entire Bible are named after a woman. Esther is one of them. (Do you know the only other book named after a woman? Answer: Ruth!)

These women must have been very important for Bible books to be named after them. Right now we're thinking about Esther. Who exactly was she?

Her story has much to teach us about

God and about ourselves. But, like so many of the best stories, Esther's didn't begin as a happy one. We quickly learn that Esther was an orphan—she had no father or mother. Maybe you know how hard it is to lose someone you love. Maybe you've lost a parent or a grandparent or a friend. If so, Esther understood this kind of loss.

But God was with her and He's with you too.

So let's see what happens next.

God, I thank You for giving me Esther's story so I can read and learn from it.

A KIND COUSIN

*When her father and mother died,
Mordecai took her as his own daughter.*

Esther 2:7

Because Esther had no parents, she needed someone to love her.

The Bible tells us that Esther was raised by her cousin Mordecai. He must have been a good cousin. He must have loved Esther very much.

But this isn't all we know about Esther's early days. We also know that she was also called Hadassah. And we know that she was beautiful. Can you imagine what she looked like? She probably had long brown hair and lovely brown eyes. She may have worn clothes of deep blue, with a matching hairband and white shoes.

But do you know the most beautiful thing about Esther? Along with her cousin Mordecai, she served the one true God.

Esther's story is actually much bigger than just the one we are reading. Soon we will learn—just as Esther did—that God was the one putting together all the parts of her life. He would tell a much better story than anything Esther could ever write for herself! Even the painful parts we'll learn about later would end up being good in the end.

Esther's story reminds us that nothing is impossible with God.

God, I thank You that every detail of my life matters to You. You don't ever make mistakes.

A JEWISH GIRL

Esther had not told who her people or her family were because Mordecai had told her to say nothing.

ESTHER 2:10

Have you ever kept an important secret? Maybe you planned a special gift for someone you love. And you couldn't say anything until the right time. You wanted it to be a surprise.

It can be really hard to keep a secret, can't it?

Esther had a very important secret. She was Jewish—which simply means she was born to parents from Israel. Remember, the Israelites were God's special people.

In the Old Testament, the first part of the Bible, God had a very special love for Israel and the Jewish people. But not all people agreed with God.

Being who God made you to be is a good thing. But sadly, when Esther was growing up, many people wanted to hurt the Jews. They could be in danger. So to protect her, Esther's cousin Mordecai told her she could not tell people about that part of her life.

Esther didn't tell anybody she was Jewish.

But God knew. That's how He made her. Being Jewish and loving God would be some of the most important parts of Esther's story. Let's keep reading to see why.

You had a plan for Esther from the beginning, God. You have a good plan for me too. Thank You.

THE STORY UNFOLDS

In those days King Ahasuerus sat on the king's throne in the city of Susa.

ESTHER 1:2

The book of Esther never mentions God's name. Can you believe it?

That may seem strange to us. But we know that the whole Bible is the story of God. As a book of the Bible, Esther is part of God's story too.

So we get to look for clues that God is still very much a part of the story—just as He's part of your story.

And if we look closely, we will find Him everywhere!

One important clue that lets us know God is in this story is that He allowed Esther, a Jewish girl, to live in the land of Persia. She lived in the capital city of Susa. The time was the third year of the reign of King Ahasuerus.

God chose Esther to live in a specific place at an exact time for a special purpose.

But what does all this have to do with Esther's story?

God, help me to look for You in the details of my life. Help me never to think that You are not there.

THE BEAUTY CONTEST

A ROYAL FEAST

In the third year of his rule, [Ahasuerus] gave a special supper for all his princes and leaders. The army captains of Persia and Media, the important men and princes of the many parts of the country were there with him.

ESTHER 1:3

King Ahasuerus ruled the land of Persia where Esther and her cousin Mordecai lived. The king ruled over 127 areas from India all the way to Ethiopia.

He was known for many things. Ahasuerus had many enemies. He commanded tough punishment on people who made him angry. He liked to spend lots of money.

In the third year of his reign he decided to hold two very important feasts.

These were not just any old dinner like

the ones you enjoy at Thanksgiving or Christmas. They were feasts that would last for 187 days. Can you imagine a party that goes on for six months?

King Ahasuerus wanted everyone to know how powerful and important he was. His kingdom was big and his power even bigger. He wanted to show off his power like a shiny new toy.

But things were about to go terribly wrong.

And God's big plan for Esther's life was about to unfold.

God, I know that people in power may make bad choices. But You are still in control. I can always trust You.

AN ANGRY KING

But Queen Vashti would not come when the king sent his servants to bring her. So the king became very angry and his anger burned within him.

ESTHER 1:12

King Ahasuerus wanted to show off everything he owned. So on the last day of the feast, he planned to show people his wife, Queen Vashti. The king called her to come out and let all the men in the crowd see how beautiful she was.

But Queen Vashti didn't like that idea at all. Her husband wasn't showing people how much he loved her. He was using her beauty to make himself feel more important.

So Queen Vashti said what nobody was ever allowed to say to King Ahasuerus. She said, "No."

Can you imagine the people's surprise? Nobody said "no" to King Ahasuerus and got away with it. They might not even live to tell about it!

The king was very angry. Remember, he was known for punishing people who made him mad. So it was no surprise that he decided Vashti could no longer be queen. She was sent away from the palace forever.

But now the king didn't have a queen. This had to be fixed right away.

God, sometimes bad people do bad things. But I know I am always safe in Your care.

THE SEARCH FOR A QUEEN

The king's servants who served him said, "Let beautiful young women be found for the king. . . . Then let the young lady who pleases the king be queen in place of Vashti." This pleased the king, and he did so.

ESTHER 2:2, 4

King Ahasuerus needed a new queen as soon as possible. But where would he find one? And how?

His royal helpers told him to search for a new wife. So they all decided to host a beauty contest to find the next queen. All the young, unmarried women who lived near the king were brought to the city of Susa.

Esther arrived at the king's palace. The man in charge there was named Hegai. He quickly saw that Esther was someone special. Hegai liked Esther because she was kind in addition to being beautiful. So Hegai gave Esther the best of everything—the best makeup, the best food, the best helpers, and the best room.

Guess how long the young women got ready for the beauty contest? A whole year!

When it was finally time for the king to make his choice, the women came to him one by one. Soon, it was time for Esther to meet Ahasuerus.

What do you think happened next?

God, You know everything that's going to happen. Thank You for never being surprised!

A BEAUTIFUL CHOICE

And the king loved Esther more than all the women. She found favor and kindness with him more than all the young women, so that he set the queen's crown on her head and made her queen instead of Vashti.

Esther 2:17

Esther was beautiful. The king saw that right away.

But here are two important things the king didn't yet know about Esther: First, she had good character. That means she did right even when nobody was watching. Having a beautiful character is far better than just having good looks.

Second, she was Jewish. And back when Esther lived, being Jewish meant people treated you badly. Sometimes, they even wanted to kill you.

God made Esther exactly who she was

supposed to be. But Mordecai had told her to keep her Jewish heritage secret. Does that remind you of any other stories in the Bible?

Remember when Moses' mother hid him in a basket floating on the Nile River? That was because he was Jewish too, and his mother wanted to protect him.

Now Esther was getting a lot of attention. She was the most beautiful girl in the whole empire. King Ahasuerus called her the winner and made her his new queen.

But was that a good thing?

God, I know You see everything I do. Help me do right even when nobody is watching.

QUEEN OF PERSIA

EVIL PLANS

In those days, while Mordecai was sitting at the king's gate, Bigthan and Teresh, two of the king's servants from those who watched over the door, became angry. And they planned to kill King Ahasuerus.

ESTHER 2:21

Esther was made the new queen of Persia. But other important things were happening too.

Cousin Mordecai was sitting by the king's gate when he heard two of the royal guards making evil plans. They wanted to kill the king! These angry guards thought they could take the power and riches that belonged to King Ahasuerus.

What would you do if you heard someone talking like that?

Mordecai decided to help, right away. He went to Esther and told her what he'd heard. Then Esther told the king.

King Ahasuerus was thankful that Mordecai had saved his life. But he soon forgot all about it!

Why was Mordecai in the right place at the right time to hear the guards talking against the king? Was it just luck? Maybe it's another clue that God was writing Esther's story.

It was God who put Mordecai in the right place. That's because God had a good plan.

What story was God writing? It would become clear very soon.

God, help me know what to do when I see people doing wrong. Give me courage to do the right thing.

A DAY TO DIE

Men were sent with letters to all the king's lands, to destroy, to kill, and to put an end to all the Jews, both young and old, women and children, in one day. This was the thirteenth day of the twelfth month, the month of Adar. And they could take the things that belonged to the Jews.

ESTHER 3:13

Exciting stories always seem to have a bad guy. Esther's story does too.

The bad guy's name is Haman.

He was a very important man in Persia. Haman was actually the second most important person in the whole kingdom, after the king himself. Haman was so important that the king commanded everyone to kneel before him.

But Esther's cousin Mordecai didn't want to kneel to Haman.

The Bible doesn't tell us just why

Mordecai refused. But it might be because Mordecai only wanted to bow to God.

Whatever the reason, Haman was mad! He tried to figure out why Mordecai wouldn't kneel before him. And Haman found out a secret: Mordecai was Jewish.

Haman knew exactly what to do to punish Mordecai. Haman went to the king and asked him to create a law to kill all the Jewish people.

Can you believe this? The king agreed!

God, there are still evil people in the world today. Give me confidence that You are with me and will protect me.

A DANGEROUS DECISION

"For if you keep quiet at this time, help will come to the Jews from another place. But you and your father's house will be destroyed."

ESTHER 4:14

Esther heard that her cousin Mordecai was very sad. So she sent a message to find out what the trouble was. Mordecai showed her the law that would kill her people.

In the most famous verse of Esther's entire story, Mordecai said to her, "Who knows if you have not become queen for such a time as this?" (Esther 4:14).

Mordecai believed God had a plan for Esther's life. Mordecai thought God had made Esther queen so she could save her people from death.

So Esther made her decision. She was

going to tell people that she was Jewish. And she would ask the king to help her people.

This sounds like a great idea, right? The king really liked Esther. What could go wrong?

Lots of things could go wrong. The law in Persia said nobody could speak to the king without a royal invitation. And breaking this law meant you could be put to death.

Esther knew that going to see the king was dangerous. She might be giving up her own life for her people.

God, when I am put in a situation where doing right is hard, help me to have courage.

WAITING FOR HOPE

There was much sorrow among the Jews in each and every part of the nation where the king's law was made known. They went without food and cried with sounds of sorrow. Many lay in cloth made from hair and in ashes.

ESTHER 4:3

Esther's people—the Jews—must have felt awful about the king's rule that they were all going to die. We know they were scared and sad because the Bible says they stopped eating and cried.

The people may have wondered if God had forgotten them. They may have asked questions like, Where is God? Is He still at work to help us? Is He really good?

Bad things happen in our lives. Sometimes the bad things happen to us, sometimes to people we love. Then we wonder many of the same things. Where is God? Is He still at work to help us? Is He really good?

But we only see part of the story. And we don't know what will happen next.

God knew that what He had planned was bigger and better than anybody could imagine. God had already made Esther, the Jewish girl, the king's wife when the Jews needed hope.

And hope was on the way.

God, You are good all the time. Help me to believe that when I have questions.

PROTECTOR OF HER PEOPLE

AN IMPORTANT DINNER

"If I have found favor in the king's eyes, and if it please the king to give me what I ask of him, may the king and Haman come to the special supper that I will make ready for them. And tomorrow I will tell you what I want."

ESTHER 5:8

Esther decided to host a special banquet. She invited two people: King Ahasuerus and Haman.

Why would she invite the enemy of her people to a fancy dinner?

At the banquet, Esther told the two men that they were invited to another banquet the next day. The men agreed to come back. Then they left for the evening.

As he walked home, Haman passed Mordecai on the street. Just like before,

Mordecai did not bow down to Haman. He was really mad! Haman thought Mordecai needed to show him more respect. Selfishness and pride made him think that way.

Haman decided to build a tower that he could hang Mordecai from. Haman would kill his enemy first thing in the morning in front of everybody.

Haman was an evil man. Things did not look good for Esther's cousin.

God, when evil men do evil things, You have not lost control. Please help me to remember that.

ONE LONG NIGHT

During that night the king could not sleep. So he had the Book of the Chronicles brought to him, and they were read to the king.

ESTHER 6:1

Something strange happened after Esther held her first special banquet for King Ahasuerus and Haman. That's the night Haman told men to build a tower to kill Mordecai on. On the same night the king couldn't sleep.

No matter what he tried, Ahasuerus stayed wide awake. So he sent his servants to go get the history books. The king wanted someone to read to him about the things that had happened during his reign. It was almost like King Ahasuerus wanted to have some bedtime stories read to him—only these stories were true.

As the servant read, he came across a story about Mordecai. Do you remember when he was sitting at the king's gate? And he overheard two guards talking about killing the king?

Ahasuerus had forgotten that Mordecai saved his life. The history books were a good reminder. Now he realized he should do something to thank Mordecai.

But what could that be?

*God, I thank You for the Bible.
I can read it and remember the
wonderful things You have done.*

THE PLAN CHANGES

Haman thought to himself, "Whom would the king want to honor more than me?"

ESTHER 6:6

The next morning the evil Haman went to the palace to ask the king for something.

Haman wanted Ahasuerus to kill Mordecai on the tower that morning.

But before he could say a word, the king asked Haman a question. "What should be done for a man whom the king wants to honor?"

Haman thought for sure the king was talking about him. Haman thought nobody in the entire kingdom was better or more important than he was.

So he answered with all the things that he would like. "Let him wear the king's clothes and ride on the king's horse all over town so people can see him."

"Good idea!" the king said. "Now, do all this for Mordecai the Jew! He is sitting at the king's gate. Do not do any less than what you have said."

Can you imagine how Haman must have felt? The man he wanted to kill was the same man the king planned to honor!

God, You are in charge of everything. Please remind me when it looks as if bad people are in control.

THE MOMENT OF TRUTH

Queen Esther answered, "If I have found favor in your eyes, O king, and if it please the king, I ask that my life and the lives of my people be saved."

ESTHER 7:3

Life didn't get any easier for Haman.

Mordecai was honored in Susa. He wore the king's clothes and rode the king's horse. And mean, selfish Haman had to lead Mordecai around town. But things were about to get even worse.

Esther soon invited King Ahasuerus and Haman back for her second banquet. When they all sat down to dinner, Esther told the king two important things. First, she let the king know that she was Jewish.

Second, she told Ahasuerus that Haman wanted to kill all of her people. Haman had created that horrible law to destroy Esther's cousin Mordecai and every other Jewish person.

This was the moment of truth. The king had to choose between Haman and Esther.

Happily, the king chose his wife. And then he sent Haman to be killed on the tower he'd built for Mordecai.

*God, please give me courage
to always tell the truth
and say the right thing.*

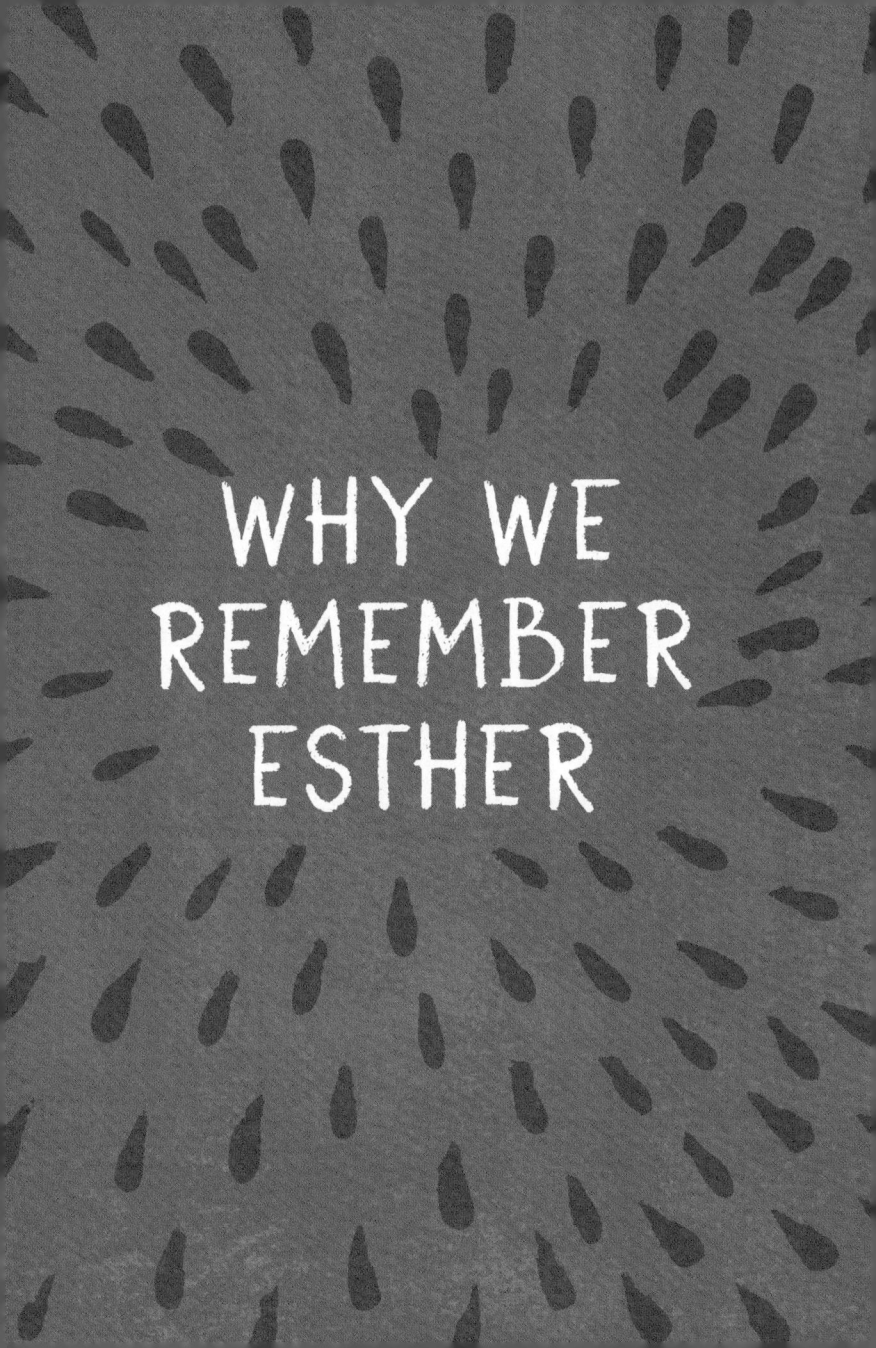

WHY WE REMEMBER ESTHER

ESTHER'S COURAGE

"Then I will go in to the king, which is against the law. And if I die, I die."

ESTHER 4:16

Esther was a brave woman.

That doesn't mean she was never scared or sad. It doesn't mean she was some perfect superhero. It just means that she wanted to please God the most. It didn't matter if that cost Esther her life.

This courage is the reason we know about Esther today. It's the reason people will keep learning about Esther forever.

There were probably many beautiful women in Persia when Esther was alive. So we don't remember Esther all these years later because of the way she looked. We remember her because of her courage. Courage to do the right thing is always more important than beauty.

Proverbs 31:30 says, "Pleasing ways lie and beauty comes to nothing, but a woman who fears the Lord will be praised."

Esther loved God and His people more than she loved herself. That's why God put her in the Bible.

But you know what? There's even more. This story isn't quite done yet.

*God, help me to love You
and Your people even more
than I love my own life.*

GOD'S RESCUE PLAN

For the Jews it was a time of joy and happiness and honor.

ESTHER 8:16

Do you remember that Haman asked the king to create a law to kill every Jewish person in Persia? When Esther told her husband what had happened, Ahasuerus was angry. He wanted to help the Jews. But once the king had made a law, it could not be changed.

The king had Haman killed. But the Jewish people still needed a rescue plan. And they needed one fast.

Mordecai and Esther worked together with the king to create a second law. This one would allow the Jewish people to fight back on the day they were to be killed.

They could defend themselves against their enemies.

And on the thirteenth day of the month of Adar, the Jewish people destroyed their enemies. Then they celebrated with the best banquets and feasts you can imagine.

Instead of death that day, the Jewish people enjoyed victory. God always has a rescue plan for the people He loves.

Sometimes the rescue doesn't go the way we want it to. But God always works His plans out for our good.

When life gets hard, God hasn't forgotten you. His rescue plan is still coming.

*God, help me to trust Your
rescue plan for my life,
especially when life is hard.*

BORN FOR THIS

"Who knows if you have not become queen for such a time as this?"

ESTHER 4:14

There are lots of people and places and happenings in Esther's story.

But here are some of the most important things. We know that Esther was born Jewish. She was beautiful. She became queen of Persia. And she was brave "for such a time as this."

Even more important, God was watching over every part of Esther's story. He didn't miss a single minute. God has promised to be with His people. And He never breaks a promise.

God's name cannot be found in the story

of Esther. But it's not hard to "see" Him all through the book. Everything that happened to Esther was under God's control.

Your story is just as important as Esther's.

God has put you on this earth, in your family, at this time. He wants to accomplish His good plans through you. Even if you never grow up to be a queen, God has big ideas for your future.

What were you born to do? Whatever it is, be brave. Stand against evil. Do what God wants, no matter what the cost.

*God, please help me to see
You all through my story.
Do good things through me.*

A HAPPY ENDING

The Jews set apart this special time each year for themselves, for their children and their children's children, and for all who joined them. They would always remember to keep these two days special, as it was written and at the same time every year.

Esther 9:27

Esther's story ends the way a good story should—happily.

God's people, the Jews, were rescued. Esther was rewarded for her courage. A new holiday called Purim was held in her honor. Mordecai took Haman's job as the second most important person in the kingdom. And God enjoyed the trust the Jews put in Him even when they were afraid.

We can trust God when we're afraid too. Sometimes we might think God has left us alone. But He hasn't. His name never appears once in the story of Esther—but God was there. He is always part of our stories too. We can see Him everywhere we choose to look.

God never, ever abandons His children. And He always keeps His promises.

He is good and He is faithful. So we can trust Him.

The very best ending to this story is if you follow Esther's example. Today, pray that God will make you a brave young woman for such a time as this.

God, please give me the courage and boldness to do what is right, every day and in every way.